me

The Power of Cultivating
and Loving the Authentic YOU!

Yah Hughes, M.Ed.

DEDICATION

Because I am so very proud of me, this one is for me,
Yah you did it, girl! Keep cultivating and loving YOU!

TABLE OF CONTENTS

PREFACE

"How did you become confident in yourself?"

IT WAS A question an audience member asked me at a women's empowerment event; I had the pleasure of being a panelist for. And instead of answering right away, I sat in silence for what seemed like forever. I was reflecting on the woman I had become and the woman she'd heard so boldly declaring how to live in her truth, to be courageous and to be everything that God created you to be. Lost in my timeline of *how* I got *here*, thinking about the thousands of times I almost didn't make it to this seat, I tried to sum up sixteen years' worth of tears, frustrations, un-learning and embracing in just one or two sentences:

> *"If I had enough time, I would tell you that it took work (a whole LOT of work) and lots of internal adjustments to get here. It took hard moments of standing in my truths and focusing on who I didn't see in the mirror in order to become who I wanted to see. So, yeah it took work...let me rephrase that, it **takes** work."*

That was the day I knew I needed to share not only my journey but the tools to help women all across the nation embrace who they are while honoring their process (past and pain) and preparing for who they're becoming.

Here is what my three sentence response didn't capture and where it all really came from.

I went through years of not fully loving and embracing who I was created to be. I didn't have a clue about the woman who was inside of me. I didn't know her power, her strength or her resilience, because the negative images painted on the walls of my environment were always surrounding me. I only believed that reflection, and it was rooted in the seeds of doubt, insecurity, and fear. My internal struggle was that I wanted desperately to be loved and because I felt that I didn't have the love I wanted, I went searching for it constantly and always came up short (I mean always, chile!). Feeling inadequate and worthless, caused me to believe I needed something "more" to feel whole and loved, and as a result, I filled my days, months and eventually years searching for an indication of my belonging, my place in life and my purpose. It was one quest after another. I was on this quest of *finding* something I should have been cultivating all along…ME!

I was looking for love in all the wrong places, and if I had just looked within - if I would have just given myself more attention, time, understanding - I would not have been on a quest for more than ten years trying to find something or even someone who I already was. This 10+ year journey led me to my purpose of teaching women how to shift their thinking about themselves, how to manage their emotions and live out their God-ordained purpose through becoming emotionally whole and cultivating an authentic positive relationship with themselves.

This book is designed to help you understand the value in cultivating and embracing *yourself*. It is intended to catapult you toward a more meaningful, healthier and more loving relationship with yourself. *Hello...Me!* will help you, whether young or old, embrace who you truly are, without fear, and make decisions on a daily basis that support this. It will provide tools to effectively love, accept, and honor yourself while becoming the best version of yourself possible. This book will challenge you to place yourself in the highest regard, with the highest priority - even when your thoughts, your circumstances, situations, and even other people, make you feel and believe you shouldn't or aren't worthy enough.

Hello…Me! is not just a "self-help book," it is a personal development tool created to help cultivate women who are on the journey to honor and love themselves unconditionally.

I believe that personal development is the key to growth, change and a true unleashing of personal power. This is your personal push to honor every part of your journey, stand in your truths and love the ugliest parts of you.

INTRODUCTION

"HELLO!" **IT'S THE** most widely used expression or offering of a greeting we give one another. Coined in the 1800s, *"hello"* was first used to attract attention or to express surprise and later evolved into America's standard greeting. It's the simplest yet perfect way to welcome, acknowledge, start a conversation with and embrace the person in front of you. Speaking of the person in front of you, have you looked in the mirror and said *hello* to the most powerful, intelligent and daring person within... YOU?

No? It's imperative that you take this opportunity to stand "naked' in the mirror and welcome the version of yourself who is staring back at you while examining what's needed to embrace the version God is shaping and molding. Saying *Hello* requires you to look beyond the surface and into the mirror of your heart and soul. It's time to stand in the mirror.

There are actually two mirrors we look into: the physical glass object that displays how well put together we are externally; the other, is an internal mirror of our inner selves reflecting the conditions of our souls. Our souls are composed of the mind, the will and emotions, and reflects who we truly are. Have you looked into the "*mirror*" of your soul and examined who's there? Can you honestly say that the woman staring back at you is the woman of your dreams? Is she the one you're proud of, and not just for her accomplishments, but for her strides of being vulnerable, bold, courageous and authentic? Or has life circumstances caused her to stop dreaming altogether? Did you allow life to cause you to live below your own expectations? Have you unapologetically welcomed and embraced every part of you? And I'm not just talking about the parts that you like, but the parts you've tucked away because you've been made to feel that they serve no purpose; the parts that make you feel less than and the parts that physically stop you from being your most true and genuine, authentic self?

Well, I have! It was the scariest, yet most exhilarating and necessary thing I've done! Sixteen years ago, I discovered the power of vulnerability, authenticity, and strength. I've since learned that fully embracing my inner self was the key to unlocking emotional healing, a life of freedom, a heart full of abundance and peace. The most intentional and powerful thing I've done was to develop and nurture the relationship with myself. Actually, I'm still learning, growing and cultivating this relationship, but for the past 16 years, I've been evaluating, unlearning, changing, cultivating, growing and loving ME!

I remember the day like it was yesterday, the day I realized my actions, my life, and my thoughts, didn't match who I was created to be. I was wrestling with who I saw and who I felt inside. One day I looked up, and I saw me - but it wasn't me. I resembled her. I could hear her even, but her voice was faint, tired, angry and unsure. It was as if I was losing her right before my eyes, and was wrestling with the thought, "do I just let her disappear into the world or do I fight to help regain her strength and put light into her?" Of course, I decided the latter. But, I almost gave her permission to leave and would have just settled for being less than the woman God created for me to be. It was easy to stay the same - to allow comfort, complacency, and excuses to be the driving force in living a mediocre life and for throwing in the towel and giving up. But I had to instead, make a decision to fight for her, to show up on the days I felt lost, unloved, unworthy, scared, shameful, confused and to go deep within to find her. And I allowed myself to feel, to change, to step out the box and fall unapologetically in love with her.

So many women won't search, find and fight for who they are truly meant to be. For who they are becoming.

They settle for comfort, and not because it's convenient but because they don't know where to begin or *how* to fight. Most women haven't decided to embrace the greatest version of themselves because they didn't know it was an option, seeing only what was placed in front of them or due to esteem issues, put themselves down to build someone else up. Well, I'm here to tell you, you are worth the fight! The fight against your fears, the fight against the old version of you, the fight against the generational curses in your family that caused you to sit and settle for less than who you are. It's time to fight, for the most authentic version of you!

Now, this fight doesn't require your fist or the neck roll. Well, maybe the neck roll. This fight is a little different though. It will require examination, vulnerability, honesty, strength, prayer, faith, and a decision. A decision to stand "naked" in the face of your flaws, your foreign parts and your fears and to no longer accept complacency, mediocrity, or any version of you that no longer serves your best interests. You have to decide that you are worth fighting for, to re-introduce yourself to the ever-changing, ever-growing versions of you.

I pray that just by you picking up this book, you are ready to get in the ring and make the decision to fight for your inner voice, your healing, your growth and well, you!

I wish I could say this journey and process has been and will be easy because it hasn't and it won't be. There have been some painful, heart-aching realities, sleepless nights and days where I wanted to give up and wanted to succumb to comfort and complacency. There were several times I entertained fear, self-doubt and just remaining unchanged. But let me tell you, I didn't, and thank God! I fought hard to become aware of who I am, and to see myself from a new lens. I fought even harder to love, honor and accept myself. And I am on a continuous journey of personal and self-development. I hope that you would join me and thousands of other women on this journey.

This is not a fairy tale love story of five steps to becoming a better you, nor is it filled with fluffy quotes and tips to help you see you differently, but it is a tool that comes as a result of prayer, faith, constant mental shifting and making intentional, deliberate, daily decisions to become a better version of yourself.

This book is for the woman who is ready to stand in the "*mirror*" of her soul, embrace authenticity and to make a conscious decision to continuously develop the relationship within. ***Hello...Me!*** is not meant to be a one-time read. It's meant to serve as a resource for you to intentionally embrace everything you are and who you have been created, by God, to be.

Here's to: standing tall in the face of all the ugly parts of you; doing the work; vulnerability; making the decision to embrace change and to embrace yourself; the soon-to-be-revealed, the real, authentic, one-of-a-kind, you! It is time to meet her face-to-face and say, ***Hello!***

PART ONE

———————

Let's take a deeper look…
evaluating what you see.

A GLANCE IN THE MIRROR

MIRRORS HAVE ALWAYS been the catalyst for my change, growth, and self-acceptance. As I look back at the pivotal moments in my life, it has always started with me standing in the mirror, face to face with myself - usually with tears in my eyes and frustration in my heart. Like the morning in 2009, when I finally had my (then, two-year-old) son ready for school and I walked into the bathroom to get myself together for work, and I looked up at the mirror, seeing this residue and cloudy film. I could see myself but it just wasn't clear, so I wiped the mirror several times and realized what wasn't clear was ME! I could see *me* in the physical sense, but Yah - the bold, the courageous, the purposeful Yah - I didn't see. I took a step back because it took my breath away. How could the "Purpose Cultivator" suddenly be in this space of not knowing who she was?

I was thriving in my career, as a wife and a mother, but it came with sacrifice, and unfortunately, the sacrifice was me. I sacrificed myself to be everything to everyone else. So, there I was, at 7:30 in the morning, trying to see myself clearly. Standing face to face with two different versions of myself, I started thinking about what I had sacrificed and where I lost myself. When did "I" leave?

When did I quiet my voice and become so enthralled with the roles in my life, that I no longer felt comfortable in my own skin? I was lost in a familiar place, not fully being able to see myself. So much had changed, yet and still, so much needed to change.

Standing in the mirror that morning allowed me to evaluate myself and what I needed to live and thrive fully. There was no devastating sequence of events that led up to that unfamiliar place. There were just infinitely small life changes that caused me not to recognize the woman staring back at me. Often, we look for major life-altering and painful experiences to cause us to reflect on who we are and what is needed. And sometimes major and painful experiences may not necessarily happen, but *life* does happen, and it causes us to be consumed with it and lose ourselves in the monotony along the way. Our lives are a long series of experiences, decisions, successes, and lessons learned. If we take time to reflect on the series and how it has added to the person we are today, we can cultivate a better relationship with ourselves. The "mirror" helps us evaluate not only the journey of life but how the journey has affected, shifted, changed and challenged us. The key is to be willing to take the moments needed to stand in the mirror, unfiltered, with just you and YOU. Being honest about who you see, how she looks, the conditions of her heart, mind, emotions and overall self are most important during this evaluation. Those intentional moments of introspect are where we begin to neglect ourselves, no longer. We know that the greatest relationship we will ever have is the one with ourselves, yet sadly it is the most neglected relationship. We spend so much time caring for everyone else and nurturing other relationships in our lives that the primary relationship, the one with ourselves, takes a backseat. And the backseat is a dangerous place to drive from. There are so many things obscuring our view, causing us to lose sight of our direction and ultimately our destination.

How long have you been driving from the backseat in your life?

No, really. Be honest and transparent with yourself for just a moment. You may even find this to be difficult, but I want you to stand in front of your mirror. Take a good long look and think. Think about your life right now and evaluate your current relationship with your *self*. Again, this may be difficult for you to do, but if you're willing, you can learn so much about you and your needs. If you were to *take inventory* of the relationship you have with YOU, how are you? What's changed or is changing with you? Have you stopped to assess what you need? How do you respond to you? In what ways have you shown up for you? Sacrifice yourself?

Imagine looking back at the end of your life and asking yourself, *how well did I love myself? Honor my commitments to me? Was I completely honest with myself? Was I my own best friend?*

It is very easy to neglect you, to give others the best parts of you, while giving yourself what's leftover. And if you aren't intentional or reflective, you'll end up living your entire life sacrificing yourself, never being who you were created and destined to be. Did you know that the majority of your life will be spent with yourself? This includes the time spent in your thoughts and feelings. Your life is spent learning about yourself...well, at least it should be.

Your life should be about living, learning and taking time to reflect, being present and looking at yourself, evaluating the way you love, learn, react and hard conversations with yourself. It's about taking the time to *check-in* regularly. This is when you intentionally ask yourself what you need and take strides to ensure that you get it. It's having those courageous and hard conversations so that you can check-in with you and learn. The best way to learn and grow is through assessment and evaluation. Evaluating yourself can help you identify where you are, how you've grown, what areas are lacking and then you can develop a growth plan as well as a plan of action to move forward. Self-assessment/reflection is designed to promote greater self-awareness and to help you identify thoughts, actions, and feelings that may be getting in the way of you living fully. This part of your journey requires that you are honest and take a conscious assessment of your behaviors. When we don't step back and assess, even while moving and pushing through life, we don't evolve. We're just going through life, unaware and unfulfilled. As a result, we get lost in roles and titles; we do things we don't want to do just to fulfill obligations, promises and to please others. We stay in jobs we should have quit long ago. We hold onto relationships that drain our energy. We settle for merely existing and not *being* the greatest versions of ourselves.

When we take time to step back and look at where we are and what is needed for our new path, we begin the process of unlearning, discovering and becoming. I read this quote by Toni Collette that says:

"The better you know yourself, the better your relationship with the rest of the world." This couldn't be any closer to the truth. Knowing who you are, actively loving you and checking in regularly to ensure your needs are met, helps you to do the same with all of your relationships and roles in your life. You are only as good to others as you are to yourself. I say this to all of my clients, "you teach people how to treat you, based on how you treat yourself AND you treat people how you treat you." Having an authentic relationship with yourself involves making sure your needs are met *first*. Authenticity requires that you prioritize you; every part of you. It also means protecting your emotional space, not subjecting yourself to perspectives, people, relationships and environments that make you feel less than or disempower you. It means taking time to look at how you show up in your head. That includes you how you show up for you, your self-talk, and self-sabotage.

DEFINING THE RELATIONSHIP
WITH YOU

JUST LIKE ANY other relationship in your life there comes a time when you might question, *what are we doing? And why?* Why are you in this relationship? What have you done to cultivate it? What value is placed on this relationship? How do you show up and contribute to this relationship? Ultimately, to thrive in any relationship, you must define exactly what the relationship is. And to do so, you must have *the* talk. I know, that awful talk that we dread because of fear - fear of the unknown, fear of the possible expectation placed on us, fear of defining and changing the relationship because we're comfortable and we don't want to deal with what defining the relationship means. However, it is necessary to be in a fully functioning and healthy, committed relationship.

As a communicator, I am always one for setting the tone, making things clear and making every attempt to understand what is expected of me and from me. I have learned over the years that I don't function well if I don't understand, know and/or grasp what is expected of me. You too may be like that, needing clear, succinct instructions, definitions and expectations. At some point in our relationship with ourselves, we must have the *talk* and define the relationship. This talk includes evaluating what you've done and how you've actively participated in the relationship with yourself. It means being honest about how you could have been better, given more and what you need to change and grow. It also means shifting from "it's complicated" to being fully committed. Committed to your own happiness, growth, change and partnering with God to live out the life destined for you. It's also about managing your expectations, the expectations you have placed on yourself without taking a moment to see if you're able to meet those expectations, whether you are healthy enough for the expectations and evaluating if those expectations are even realistic.

If you were to evaluate the relationship that you have with yourself and all the fundamental elements that go into a relationship such as understanding, respect, love, trust, honesty, and communication, can you say that you nurture each area? Have you been a good steward over you? Would you stay in this relationship if it was with someone else? I want you to take a detailed look at where you are in relation to self, and this will be your focal point as you continue cultivating, shifting, and becoming the greatest version of yourself.

In the next section we will take inventory of what you say to yourself, but before we do, take a moment to answer the following: How do you speak to yourself? Is what you're saying to yourself stopping you from choosing you or from loving you unconditionally? What are the automatic messages that seem to always be on repeat in your head?

THE POWER OF A WORD

DID YOU KNOW we have over 50,000 thoughts a day? Over half are negative, and over 90% are just repeating from the day before. Our words have power and are life forming. The way we communicate impacts the quality of our relationships and that includes how we speak to ourselves too. Self-talk refers to the ongoing internal dialogue with ourselves. It is your inner voice, comprised of your conscious and unconscious belief. Whether it's cheerful and supportive or negative and self-defeating, it is the content and the tone of what you tell yourself. Self-talk is the *what* and the *how* of speaking to yourself. Ultimately it is the conversation inside of your head and is the source of your emotions and mood. The conversations you have with yourself can be beneficial or damaging and destructive. They can influence how you react and respond to life. If I were to record the conversations you have inside your head, what would I hear? What would I learn about you? Are these conversations more positive or more on the side of negative?

Many are in the place they're in right now not because of financial instability, the wrong career choice, or because God didn't hear them, it is a direct result of how they speak to themselves. When I stood in that cloudy mirror back in 2009, reflecting on and evaluating what I saw, I had to be honest about what I was saying. My own self-talk (the way in which I spoke to myself) was not the best. I had a word playlist that supported the unfamiliar life that was staring back at me. The automatic messages in my head were that I 'didn't have *time* to focus on me' and that 'there was too much' that needed my time and attention. I had 'work to *do*' and 'I made it this far so it couldn't be that bad.' I'd say, "I'm okay" or "I will be okay."

The problem was that those automatic messages kept me *doing* something but hindered me from *being* everything. I was always doing something and because I didn't have the time - to check in *with* me, to see how I was growing and changing, and to listen to my needs and desires - I was not properly with myself. I wasn't doing the work and putting in the time I needed for me. I was diminishing where I was and telling myself that I was okay, and that kept me stagnant. I didn't realize that my inner dialogue was what plagued me. I soon had to be honest with myself and take ownership of my thoughts and recognize how they were crippling me from cultivating a better relationship with myself. Words have the power to form life whether we actually speak them or think them. Just as Proverbs 18:21 declares "*Death and Life are in the power of the tongue: and they that love it shall eat the fruit thereof.*" We must caution the thoughts that become our internal talk because it will manifest in our lives.

All day long, we're in dialogue with one person - *ourselves.* If you took a moment to evaluate your inner speech, what would you find you're saying most to *you*? Is the majority of it positive and life producing? How is your inner voice stopping you from choosing you, from moving forward and unleashing the new version of you? Does it paralyze you or propel you?

Evaluating what you say to yourself is critical and will help you move forward. I wish I could say that the majority of the women I come in contact with and have met in these "*purpose streets*" have had more positive self-talk than negative, but that doesn't hold true. So many struggle with the conversations they have with themselves. Negative self-talk is defeating and destroying, and it happens when you replay upsetting or damaging events over and over again. Make no mistake; negative self-talk doesn't always show up in a bold way. It can be passive aggressive. It's the inner critic or like one of my favorite authors Brene Brown, says, it's "*your gremlin.*" This voice can be sweet and loving one minute and the next, an evil, destructive villain. It's the "Negative Nancy" in your own mind, and *she* can be harsh and abrasive, preventing you from living fully.

There are four types of negative self-talk, and you may struggle with one, if not more, of these types:

1. Filtering: You magnify only the negative aspects of the situation.

2. Personalizing: When something bad happens you automatically blame yourself.

3. Catastrophizing: You automatically attempt and assume the worst.

4. Polarizing: You see things only as either good or bad, with no middle ground. It's either perfect or a total failure.

Learning how your inner critic or *gremlin* shows up is key to shifting the conversation because we cannot conquer what we do not confront and we can no longer deal with just the symptoms and not the root cause. No matter how it shows up for you, here are some ways you can begin to combat the inner critic and shift the conversation within.

Tools to combat negative self-talk:

1. Check yourself: Now that you have identified *how* it shows up be intentional in stopping yourself *when* it happens. This is not going to be easy, so repetition is key.

2. Put it into perspective: Is this situation as bad as I'm making it? What is the worst thing that could happen? How likely is it?

3. Challenge it: What is the evidence for or against my thinking? Is it factual or just my interpretation?

4. Shift your focus: begin to look at the good and positive in the situation and begin to reframe your mind to no longer immediately go for the negative.

These tools will help you begin the process of reframing, identifying, challenging and putting things into perspective as they relate to the way you speak to yourself and silencing your inner critic. Changing habitual ways of thinking can be hard and a huge undertaking especially if you've been doing it for a very long time. The key is to be consistent and intentional with learning new ways to talk to ourselves realistically. To effectively reframe your thinking and self-talk, consider who you're trying to become and focus on how to speak to and encourage her.

When you begin to shift the way you speak to yourself, you're able to begin then to get a better handle on self-sabotage. Unfortunately, negative self-talk and self-sabotage go hand in hand. I call them the dysfunctional twins, *Negative Nancy & Debbie Downer*. Most times you don't experience one without the other. To shift from the "Nancy and Debbie," you have to dig deep within your mind and combat both. Now that we've covered Nancy let's get into Miss Debbie, also known as self-sabotage. Whether you refer to it as *self-sabotage* or getting in your own way, *it's the act of destroying or damaging something deliberately so that it does not work correctly.* Many people live in self-made prisons; prisons of fear, doubt, resentment, and negative thoughts. All of these things become stories in their minds that have limited them from achieving greatness because they've rehearsed them so much, there's no clear distinction between the made up stories and reality.

We spend a great deal of time in self-sabotage mode by imagining scenarios that don't exist or never happened, making up stories in our minds that are engulfed in fear and persuaded by worry about the future.

Self-sabotaging thoughts and behaviors are perpetuated by your inner critic. It comes from fear and limiting beliefs. Self-sabotage is used to keep you confined and in bondage. It is a wound that manifests in your thoughts and actions. It is any action that gets in the way of your intent.

Self-sabotage can show up in subtle or even complex and destructive ways. Subtle ways normally start off as small meaningless behaviors that get in the way of a long term goal. This may look like, eating cake, knowing you've committed to a healthy lifestyle. Complex and destructive ways may manifest as constantly comparing yourself to others, procrastination, and self-medicating with drugs and/or alcohol, to name a few. We tell ourselves stories of how we *can't*, are *less than*, need *more* in order to keep us limited, safe and from failing. We self-sabotage for various reasons: familiarity with failure, to avoid disappointment and rejection, as an unconscious need for control, feelings of unworthiness but particularly because it's safe and comfortable. Sabotaging ourselves often takes on the form of protection. It can hide behind impulsiveness or even manifest as indecisiveness. We think that by staying in this place and this space, that we are safeguarding ourselves from hurt and danger, but in actuality, it hinders our progression. It stops us from living the life that God intends and has blessed us with. When we sabotage, we aren't in the place of reception and cannot move to the place of authenticity. This behavior does more than stops us from moving forward. It sabotages:

- Our connection with ourselves
- Our confidence
- Our ability to succeed
- Our time
- Our relationship with God

It is imperative that you stop inventing ways to quit, to stay small, not show up, and to stay stagnant. Begin to fight your self-sabotaging behaviors by:

- First, being kind to yourself. You have to hold yourself kindly and give yourself the same grace that you extend to others. That means being less harsh with yourself and taking the time to decompress and listen to your emotions, your heart, and your body.

- The next thing you can do to fight your sabotaging behaviors is to identify and acknowledge what is causing you to sabotage yourself, get to the root of the feeling, reason and then make the changes needed to stop those behaviors.

• Lastly, take time to find and cultivate your positive inner voice. Begin to affirm yourself and have a few go-to positive reinforcements on hand, at your disposal.

The thought of change often makes us feel anxious because it means that we must challenge familiar behaviors and attitudes that we've held about ourselves. Remember that reflection is key to progression. You must be honest with yourself, knowing how you respond, what you need, and the things that are limiting you. Then, begin taking steps to work on them. Remember, checking-in with you is a powerful tool and must be a part of your process in order to continue the journey of becoming the authentic version of you. Saying *hello* means that you are brave enough to no longer run from what is presented in the mirror but instead, learn from what it reveals and welcome the changes ahead. It is liberating when we can stand tall and face ourselves in the mirror, without fear, and without feeling the need to run away, fast!

The key is that you have to take a moment to stand in the mirror, unfiltered, just you and YOU.

REFLECTION

Taking time to step back and look into the mirror of your thoughts, emotions, mind, heart behaviors and beliefs is the first and most important part of becoming the authentic version of you. It provides perspective, improves self-awareness and facilitates a deeper connection with self and learning you.

The process requires you to **STOP, LOOK, LISTEN and ACT.**

STOP doing busy work, filling your day with tasks and driving from the backseat of your life.

LOOK at your life right now, what is the driving force? Look at the conditions of your relationship with yourself, identify what needs to be nurtured, changed, embraced or eliminated to become the greatest version of you.

LISTEN to your thoughts and begin to reframe them. Listen to what God is saying to you through these moments and experiences.

ACT! It's time to identify the steps needed to move to the next phase of your journey. In what ways do you need to readjust, change, improve or grow?

PRAYER

Lord, thank you for the desire to reflect and to look within. Thank you for the work you are doing in me and my life. I praise you for keeping me when my thoughts, actions, and deeds did not align with who you created me to be. Forgive me, for allowing my thoughts to stop me from seeing you inside of me. Lord, I am grateful you think so much of me, so much more than I think of myself. Help me to see what you see, to renew my mind and my inner talk. Father, help me to think of things that honor you and myself. I declare Philippians 4:8 over my inner thoughts and I will commit to regularly reflecting on my life, actions, and thoughts. In Jesus' name, I pray. Amen.

PART TWO

Learning How to Cultivate You

Hello…ME.

Often, it's not about becoming a new person but becoming the person you were meant to be, and already are, but don't know how to be. ~ Heath L. Buckmaster

I fell in love with the cultivation process, about six years ago after researching seeds and growth for a sermon. To cultivate - means to foster growth, to improve by steady labor and care. The process of cultivation is the act of digging into or cutting up an existing soil bed to better prepare it for planting and growth. It specifically aims to get the soil into a healthy state to produce quality crops. For centuries, we as humans have been learning the process of cultivating crops, to produce quality food sources. We discovered new ways to foster growth and produce with our seeds, plants, and crops. The reason we cultivate is to help plants grow better, to develop a longer and more sustainable harvest.

This process intrigued me and had me thinking, what if we developed an agriculture mindset to cultivate the inner parts of ourselves? How can I begin to help people, women specifically, to cultivate an authentic and loving relationship with themselves? As I began to throw myself into studying that process, I started seeing my cultivation process, and how imperative it had been to the woman I am today.

Cultivate- to foster growth; to improve by labor, care, and study

To cultivate oneself means to give yourself what you need not just to get through or to survive but to produce a harvest in your inner world and thrive authentically. Cultivation is a two-fold process of learning and maintaining. It is comprised of looking inward, learning how you show up internally, fostering growth and maintaining those areas you've worked hard to nurture.

The first part of cultivation is studying or diagnosing the soil. The type of soil dictates when and how we cultivate. It's taking a detailed look at the soil to learn it. In this case, you are the soil, the fertile ground that God created to blossom and grow, but to do so, you have to study yourself. It's taking the time to look inward to understand what's going on inside of you so that you can flourish outwardly. Cultivating yourself means that you put in the work to learn who you truly are, that you feed and nurture those parts of you that need attention, and that isn't producing so that you can continue the growth process.

LOOKING INWARD

THERE ARE SEVERAL realizations I had once I began my cultivation process and developed an understanding of who I am. I realized that I had too many perceptions in my head of who I was and who I was supposed to be. I struggled with my authentic voice and being true to myself because of those voices telling me about ME. This caused so much internal conflict; I felt lost, frustrated and confused.

Have you ever felt lost, or not quite like yourself? Yes? We all have. And if we're completely honest about it, it doesn't feel good. It's a scary place to be. It can lead us down dark roads and crazy paths, the kind that will have us trying to second guess everything we know and on an unrealistic quest to "find" ourselves. Why unrealistic? Well, "finding ourselves" is what we, in my hometown of Philadelphia, refer to as a "dummy mission." How can we try to find someone we already are? That doesn't sound too smart right? I know, I have said it aloud several times, and it still doesn't make sense. So many gurus have told you that you must find yourself to be free, to be happy and to be whole but that would mean that you weren't created with purpose and intention. The concept of "finding" oneself indicates that you're lost, but I'd like to challenge that perspective and ask, are you lost or do you need to be (re)introduced to the person you're becoming after life has taught you a few things? On this road, you may have fallen out of touch with your true self and become unsure, but understanding that your identity is set, sealed and secure, is key. While you may not recognize yourself due to the direction, circumstances, and emotions you're experiencing; it's not because of your identity. Instead, place the focus on who you are, paying attention to your core and cultivating who she is.

One of the most beautiful things you will ever experience in life is when you begin to learn and uncover the person you were created to be all along - the person God intended for you to be when He first had the thought to place you into your mother's womb. This was just as he stated in **Jeremiah 1:5** *"Before I formed you in the womb I knew you, before you were born I set you apart; I appointed you as a prophet to the nations."* God affirmed Jeremiah, letting him know that he was never lost, never an accident, that he was carefully created and planned and so are you. But immediately following God's affirmation, Jeremiah made an excuse based on his prior experiences and beliefs and said in verse 6, *"Alas, Sovereign Lord, I said, "I do not know how to speak, I am too young."* Just like Jeremiah, we often look from the lens of circumstances, experiences and of others, to validate us, so it is very easy to not fully embrace our authentic selves.

We spend a great deal of time trying to be someone or something that we aren't. We measure ourselves by standards set by people who don't know us, didn't create us, and who haven't the slightest clue as to what we've been through. But, it is when we can step back and truly look on the inside of us - beyond all the noise, the clutter, and the standards set before us - that we truly can learn to uncover and embrace the greatest version of ourselves. That is called soul evaluation, and it's the *soul evaluation* that is going to free us. When we take time to learn, understand and evaluate our core, we're able to understand what we need to flourish. Who we are is unveiled when we take an intricate look at who we are not. 3 John 1:2 tells us ***"Beloved, I pray that in all respects you may prosper and be in good health, just as your soul prospers."*** We take time to cultivate, plan and grow our careers, our friendships, relationships, businesses and everything else, but God desires that we don't negate or forget about our souls. It's the voice we must recognize and adhere to when everything else doesn't line up when we don't see what God says about us. With thousands of voices telling us who to be, how to act and what to do, it is crucial that we know and understand the first and most critical part of cultivating an authentic *you*, and that is to get to know YOU.

So, Who are you?

Most of us, if given the opportunity to answer this question, would babble off a list of roles, responsibilities, and accomplishments that we believe make us who we are. While these things are great, they don't make you who you are. This question instead, is referring to your core, the unseen components inside of you that make you who you really are. This question is asking that you take a look inward, evaluating your beliefs, your emotions, and your values. This is true self-discovery. This is what it's all about — knowing and understanding what makes you-*you* and developing a better understanding of yourself. The real you. In counseling, we call it a person's "real self," and it's who you are when you release all the labels, judgments and stories that you've told yourself. It's releasing the pretenses and removing the masks. There are so many people telling you to "be yourself," but usually this statement is never accompanied with instructions or tools on how to do so. There is a lot to unpack with "being yourself." It's all about cultivating self-discovery.

Self-discovery is the process of becoming aware of one's own character and true potential. It is another way of saying "*knowing yourself.*" Honestly, it's a lifelong journey of exploration of our inner selves and allows us to really get to know ourselves. Self-discovery gives us the courage to live life exactly how we were meant to live, by being true to our core values and making peace with them. It gives us the chance to fall in love with ourselves over and over again.

Lately, there has been so much emphasis on cultivating "self-love" in our culture and especially on social media. Things like, "*love yourself more,*" "*you are enough,*" and "*until you begin to love and value yourself, you can't love anyone else*" –all of which are true, but they fail to explain the "HOW?". How do you get to the place of choosing yourself? How do you begin viewing yourself in a way that promotes love, helps you see beyond the mistakes, fear, doubt, and allows you to truly embrace your true self? Embracing *you* doesn't just happen; it's the result of continuously doing the work. You have to work to understand and discover *you* more and more. It's working through the resistance and showing up when it's painful, and you want to retreat. To cultivate a better relationship with you and to love yourself more, you have to *understand* you. Understanding *you* means that you have to take a detailed look inside of your mind, your heart, your emotions, and values and begin to find the "*why?*". Why do you think, believe, and act the way that you do? It's the act of pinpointing where your perspectives and viewpoints stem from. It's getting to the root cause of your actions and responses. Plain and simple, it's about knowing who you are. Knowing who you are is vital to the foundation and cultivation of the relationship. This concept is beyond determining your favorite food or your favorite color; it is the process of understanding who you are beyond the surface. It brings you face-to-face with some very deep-rooted things, and it makes you take a serious look at the way you show up in the personal relationship you have with yourself. It means respecting your own values, beliefs, emotions, and habits and it also means understanding your strengths, your weaknesses, what makes you come alive, and what makes you hide away.

I know that this seems overwhelming and you're probably questioning why you may not know all of these things already, but let me stop you from going down the road of self-sabotage because I know you've already started second guessing yourself and even considered putting this book down because it's intense. You don't get to knowing yourself by simply being born and going through life. Nope! You get there by making consistent, conscious efforts in evaluating, learning and being intentional about taking time to be with *you*. So take a deep breath, breathe freely, and let's continue…

ARE YOU PROPERLY IDENTIFIED?

ASKING OURSELVES "WHO am I?" is hard. It requires deep reflection at the core of our identity and an in-depth look at how we perceive ourselves. Self-Identity is imperative to this journey of cultivation. Self-identity is defined as, the natural occurring qualities that make us who we are as individuals and the recognition of one's potential and qualities as an individual.

It is the answer to the following questions:

- Who am I?

- What does it mean to be me?

- What is my biggest strength? My biggest weakness?

- What do I believe in?

- What are my values?

"Developmentally, we wrestle with finding ourselves as teens and young adults. Then we often revisit these questions in middle age. It is both normal and essential to seek self-understanding. To accept ourselves and establish a sense of belonging, we need to understand who we are. A strong sense of self, helps us navigate life and brings meaning to our experiences. Without it, we feel lost."

- Sharon Martin

Identity is a combination of our basic values that dictate the choices we make. Identity is made up of our core beliefs. Over time, we have allowed our experiences, and more often than not, our painful ones, to become the lens from which we look at ourselves, thus we begin to believe that we are the sum of our pain, our mistakes, our failures, and our doubts, instead of believing what God has said about us. Usually, negative beliefs come from negative experiences. We then become fixated on those experiences and then suffer from an identity crisis. We suffer identity crisis because we believe our identity is found in parts of us we find to be negative – things like, what we do, physical features, and social or relationship statuses. How we view ourselves is not based on our life's circumstances, issues, etc., it is based upon who we are and whose we are. If you don't know who you are, you can not properly and fully love YOU.

For so many years my own identity was wrapped up in my childhood experiences and my painful past. This was the lens in which I viewed life - rejected, broken, angry, and bitter. I told myself, I was what happened to me and I believed that I was beyond repair, so I made decisions and built a life framed around those beliefs and that identity. My relationships did not respect or honor me, because I didn't see a woman worth honoring or respecting. Life for me was based on survival and my need for attention and validation. After all, it was better than what I had received, so why not? My expectations were low, and I played small only going after things that were comfortable, familiar and in my control. Control was a big part of it for me, and I always needed it in every situation, to feel safe and secure. The interesting thing was, I knew there was more. I knew that there was another way of doing things, another way of life, but I didn't believe that I was worthy of it or having it for myself.

Instead of dreaming of a new life, I lived in the reality of my own. Now, I had always heard that '*I was the apple of God's eye, I was no accident, I had a purpose, I "would" be somebody,*' but I didn't believe it. Pain has a way of making us believe that *"this is as good as it gets"* and we shouldn't want more because after all, at least we "survived." So, we succumb to the identity of our dark places instead of leaving and creating a place full of light. We believe the negative identities more than we believe God and the positive ones because we think it's too hard to attain. But can I tell you, a new identity isn't something you have to attain, it is, however, something you step into and believe. It wasn't until I began to question my dark places, crying out in desperation, that I began to embrace a new identity, because I had to see if what God was saying was true of me. It turns out, it was true and always has been! I am ENOUGH, and so are you! Don't accept anyone else's definition of you...even if it's your own pain!

I loved me enough to finally stop going in circles, settling for bad relationships, and playing small to fit in and be accepted. I hope that you will take an opportunity to stop looking for something that you already have and begin embracing and cultivating the greatest parts of you. Self-discovery is like working out, it gets easier to do, the more consistent you are in doing it.

Self-discovery means many things. For some, it means:

- Taking the first step in actually answering the *Who am I, really?* question

- Digging deep into your past and discovering experiences that have shaped you

- Going back to the scriptures and understanding what God has said about you

- Taking some much needed time away from the soul clutter, the brain running, the life-noise and sit alone, in quiet with just YOU

For others, it means rediscovering that person you've already taken time to cultivate because you find that you don't fully recognize her anymore. **In this case**, it may require asking yourself a new question...*Who am I now?*

Now that I no longer identify with the pain, now that I have experienced significant changes, am no longer interested in being consumed or defined by my roles in life, who is this new person I've become? Have I taken the time to study the different version of myself?

Now that you've lived through life's pivots and changes, the loss, the relationship ending, motherhood, marriage, etc. and introduced to new perspectives, ideas, and feelings and realize that you are not the same person, you must stand back in the mirror and ask new questions. It's time to examine what's different with the changes that have occurred in your life. How has this impacted you? Has it changed you? Think about the differences between who you were and who you are becoming. What has contributed to these differences? How will the coming months and years transform your life? What does the new you need?

I can remember struggling with who I was after I no longer identified with my pain, my past and after I had gone through life. I was wiser, I was different, I was evolving, and that version required that I paid attention to my wants and needs. It was about me releasing ideas of who I thought I was based on old places my heart and mind had been. I had to use new tools, pay closer attention to this version, and the scope of my lens changed. The scope of your lens is vital to what you believe, and a lack thereof. Asking new, hard questions is important to your growth. Whatever those questions are for you at this present moment in your life, take time to discover who you are today. It may also mean that you take a hard look at what you ultimately believe about yourself.

YOU ARE WHAT YOU BELIEVE

I HAVE ASKED countless women this question, and now I'm going to ask you the same:

> ### *If you could be the woman of your dreams, who would you be?*

Take a moment and really reflect on this question. I'm sure you could list all of the great things you would do, what you'd look like, and have. I often hear things like, 'she would be brave,' 'more confident, not relying on others,' 'she would go after everything that she wanted.' Hearing statements like these are incredible, and I always get excited about the potential I see in women all across the world, truly living in their purpose and being everything that they desire to be. But there's a second part to that question, and the answer always puts me in the hard face of reality as to why I do what I do. It's why I'm called to coach women about self-development and emotional wholeness. The second part of that question is, *"Why aren't you, her?"* The answer is typically not typical, silence. A room with so many women, so much potential, so much to say, usually falls completely silent and I soon realize that their responses reflect their own self-belief. Well, it's not usually *their beliefs* per se, but instead, the projections placed upon them from others, have become their reality.

How you view yourself is the cornerstone of your actions, goals, dreams, and your ability to thrive. Your behavior is an indicator of your beliefs. Beliefs have the power to both create and paralyze you. A limiting belief is one that causes life to be less than completely satisfying. It causes you to second guess who you are and what you're capable of. Living based on your limits robs you of freedom, of authenticity, and of abundance.

Every time we say or think to ourselves, *I am not:*

- pretty enough

- smart enough

- funny enough

- successful enough

...we are denying that we are fearfully and wonderfully made, which in essence is denying GOD, our creator. Ouch! I know, it stung when I understood this as well. You are ENOUGH! You are more than the restrictions placed on you, even if those restrictions are self-inflicting.

Shifting our self-belief doesn't happen overnight. It

starts with going to our Creator, the person who believed in our lives so much that He created us. It then continues with us. We have to intentionally take steps to change how we view ourselves. We have to do the work. We can begin by understanding that our levels of self-belief are not set in stone; they are not final. We can then learn a new way of viewing ourselves. To shift our self-belief, we must examine the limiting beliefs. Ask yourself, *where did it come from? Whose belief is it? Is it the belief of my parents, a friend, possibly a teacher, coach or even a mentor? How has it caused me to live? Could it have been a thought planted by the enemy to make me fester on it for years and not live out my fullest potential?*

Once you've identified the source of the limiting beliefs, acknowledge that they are beliefs and not truths. Beliefs are conditioned perceptions that are built upon old memories of both pain and pleasure. These memories are based upon how you have interpreted your experience. Beliefs are ultimately assumptions we make about ourselves, others and how we expect things to be in the world around us. They are not truths, and you must realize they are not from God or even yourself, so stop honoring them! To no longer adhere to or honor your limiting beliefs, you must remove them. Discard the assumptions you have about yourself and replace them with a new belief, one that is true and supports who you are and also propels you into who you're *growing* to be. Your beliefs must aid in you flourishing, becoming greater and seeing who God created. Freedom is right on the other side of those limits.

Years ago while researching, I came across a powerful story by an unknown author, about living in freedom. This story touched me so much that I want to share it with you:

THE FREED PRINCESS

IN A DARK *castle lived a princess who had never seen her reflection. She'd been locked up her whole life, until one day she found that the door to her palace dungeon had accidentally been left open. Amazed, she stepped free for the first time. She walked outside and down to a shimmery lake - another thing she had never seen before. With wonder, she peered into the lake and, for the very first time, saw her own reflection. But it was stormy, the wind was whipping the water, and her reflection was fractured and warped.*

Naturally, the princess believed this was how she really was, how she really looked. Jagged. Distorted. Ugly. She began to cry at the 'true nature' of herself. Then a serene elderly lady quietly approached her with a kind smile and warm, understanding eyes. The lady comforted the princess and, as she gently reassured her, the warping wind calmed. Almost instantly, the surface of the lake became even and calm. The sun emerged, and everything felt gentle and peaceful once more. After a moment, the old lady encouraged the princess to observe herself again in the reflection of the now calm lake.

With everything - the elements, her mind, and the very atmosphere - calm and balanced, she now saw herself

as she truly was and started to come to know herself.
— *Anonymous*

It is my prayer that you find the *Freed Princess* inside of you and that you will take as long as you need to free her, cultivate and embrace who she truly is. It takes courage, discipline, and risk to free the princess within!

A new identity isn't something you have to attain; it is, however, something you step into and believe

REFLECTION

Take some time, before you go on to Part Three, to process and journal your experience with Part Two.

- What stood out the most?

- If you had to answer "Who am I?" what would be your response?

- What is one thing you can begin doing now to help you with self-discovery?

- What is one thing you can celebrate that you've discovered about yourself?

- What is one belief you need to change?

- What is your takeaway from *"The Freed Princess"*?

PRAYER

Father, thank you for understanding who I am and for who you created me to be. I am an heir. I am the apple of your eye. I praise you, Father, for I am fearfully and wonderfully made. Lord, help me to uncover my identity and know that it comes from you, not my past, not my pain and not my circumstances. As I awaken the greatest parts of me, give me the strength to heal, to grow and blossom into the woman you've created. As you uncover and expose the things I need to change, give me the courage to continue, not to run, not to revert back to what is familiar, and to instead be brave enough to start my journey of saying hello to the *me* you've purposed and predestined. Give me strength when it becomes too much. Give me wisdom when I don't understand. Send people who will hold me accountable. Provide resources and relief during this process Lord. I trust you, and I am fully committed to becoming the greatest version of myself. I surrender to your will for my life. I am ready to be FREED. In Jesus' name, I pray. Amen.

PART THREE

Embracing The Power of Being You

Did you know that most women spend a great portion of their everyday life in self-criticism?

Whether it is about our looks, our accomplishments, or our feelings, we spend far too much time finding fault within ourselves. In a report released by Weight Watchers (2016), women were found to criticize themselves at least *eight times* a day. In a survey of 2,000 women, one in seven participants admitted to criticizing or berating themselves regularly each day. Most of their self-criticisms dealt with weight issues, physical attributes, career paths, money, and relationships. In fact, a staggering 89 percent said that they prefer complimenting *other* women but not themselves. The survey also found that around 42 percent of women claimed that they never compliment themselves, while 58 percent gave themselves positive thoughts only once a day. Of the respondents, 60 percent admitted to having days in which they criticize themselves constantly throughout the day.

Ouch! No wonder it's so hard for women to have an authentic relationship with themselves, we can't stop beating ourselves up! It is easy to get caught up in doubting our abilities and picking ourselves apart. I too struggled with authenticity and loving the best and worst parts of me. When I started my journey of healing and embracing me 16 years ago, I didn't know much about myself. I thought that because I was 24, I knew myself, and it turned out that was the furthest from the truth. My age and life experiences didn't mean that I knew myself, let alone embraced myself. I spent more time criticizing myself instead of embracing who I was, what God made and who I was becoming. I didn't need the world to beat me up because I was already doing a great job.

When I realized that I did more damage to myself than anybody else in my life, I knew it was time for a change. Embracing me meant that I no longer got to criticize and pick myself apart. It meant that I would no longer hide behind defense mechanisms and my childhood pain, that I had to shift from identifying as the victim in my story. Choosing to embrace and develop myself took courage, strength, and vulnerability. I had to stand up close and personal with my behaviors, emotions, and shame. There was a lot of compassion and positive self-talk to help me look beyond who my mind convinced me I was and to embrace the authentic me. That *me* is brave, strong, funny, confident yet flawed, sarcastic, and a tad pushy. But, honesty and compassion were at the forefront of that process which allowed me to celebrate the great parts of myself while working on the not-so-great parts. The process took time to cultivate a genuine like and regard for myself. I made a choice daily, to honor my commitment to growth and healing, and to choosing authenticity every day for the rest of my life. Choosing authenticity means: cultivating the ability to be imperfect, allowing yourself to be vulnerable, and setting boundaries.

Embracing yourself isn't a tangible thing. It's not something you can run out and get, and it's not a checklist of things to do. Embracing you is about acceptance - accepting who you are, while still evolving. Embracing your authentic self requires you stand in the mirror welcoming the not-so-great parts that you've discovered; it's choosing to be vulnerable. It's dodging your reflection in the mirror no more, and instead standing tall, making no apologies for what you've endured and encountered. It means that you do not pull yourself apart after you've evaluated you and see what's needed in order to grow. It also means that you don't internalize the things that are meant to show you how to move forward. *Embracing you* requires that you **STOP!** Stop shaming, stop focusing on the negative, stop repeating destructive patterns, and stop conforming to your pain. When you embrace the person staring back at you, you can see her strengths, her struggles, and her strides and begin to accept every part of her.

Self-acceptance involves self-understanding, a realistic awareness of one's strengths and weaknesses. It looks like making conscious and continuous decisions to value you, to honor you, your feelings, your health, your wealth and well-being before anyone else's. Embracing your authentic self means that you maintain a certain resemblance to your feelings, needs and actions. It's dropping your need for perfection, and celebrating progress, no matter how big or small, because you understand what it took to make that tiny step. It's loving the person you've come to know as flawed, but still worthy. It's the power of owning your story - every part of it. It's knowing that you are an active part of your story, of your evolution and becoming. It's seeing what God sees and says about you. It's a commitment to becoming the version of you that God carefully planned and purposed. It's you partnering with God to be who he's created you to be. The version He describes in Jeremiah 1:5 ***"Before I shaped you in the womb, I knew all about you. Before you saw the light of day, I had holy plans for you: A prophet to the nations — that's what I had in mind for you."*** and Ephesians 2:10 ***"For we are God's masterpiece. He has created us anew in Christ Jesus, so we can do the good things He planned for us long ago."*** Choosing to embrace authenticity can be hard, but it's worth it...you're worth it. You are worthy! Worthy of living an authentic and meaningful life, worthy of trusting yourself, owning your power and seeing who you will become. Embracing *you* can be scary, but the benefits of doing so far outweigh the benefits of not being your authentic self.

"*Authenticity is the daily practice of letting go of who we think we are supposed to be and embracing who we actually are.*"

—*Brené Brown*

KEYS TO EMBRACING YOU:

EMBRACING YOU IS a choice, one you make every single day, in every single moment for the rest of your life. Practice, commitment, and consistency is the key to truly growing and embracing you. Just like your physical muscles, in order to strengthen them, you must exercise daily to see results. The same is true for your self-love and personal growth. Here are a few keys to helping you on this journey of embracing you:

KEY #1 CHOOSE YOU

So often we want to be chosen - for the job, the award, the part, the organization, and the relationship. There's nothing wrong with wanting to be chosen, but make sure you're not doing more to be chosen by someone else than you commit to choosing yourself. Choose you now and forever.

Years ago I had a training for a new system at work and the trainer instructed us to *commit and commit often.* He explained that by doing so, not only do we become familiar with the new data, we now have it saved to our hard drive and it will be programmed within. For some of us, we need to commit to choose us and choose ourselves often, repeatedly until it becomes a part of our normal practice. Choose you!

Key #2 Allow yourself to be a work in progress

Did you know that you are both a masterpiece and a work in progress? That's right, you are! You are God's masterpiece. I know sometimes that's a difficult thought to embrace and understand, but you are. A masterpiece isn't perfect but it is *perfected* with time. Understand that you will never be perfect (except in God's eyes) because you will always be a work in progress. Being a work in progress is a great thing because it means that you are not "finished", that you are still developing, growing and striving to be a better version of yourself. Release the standard of perfection and having to be a specific way by a certain time. Give yourself permission to be a work in progress, not based upon a specific time or standard, but specific to your own developmental needs.

Key #3 Forgive Yourself

Are you holding onto anger, resentment, guilt or shame toward yourself? Are you beating yourself up for not being the best mom, wife, daughter, friend or person? **Stop!** Seriously, release yourself from the mistakes, the expectations, the shame and guilt of it all. Let it go; it's not serving you. It's keeping you in a vicious cycle of hurt, stagnation, and pain. To forgive means to grant relief from, and to cease to feel resentment. When you don't forgive you place yourself in bondage, and if you're serious about cultivating a better relationship with self, you have to forgive, so it doesn't impede your progress. Forgiveness frees you and promotes healing and wholeness within. Give yourself grace and forgive yourself, not just once but as many times as you need to. Forgiveness allows you to live beyond your pain.

KEY #4 GIVE YOURSELF COMPASSION

For many of us, our default setting is to be critical and judgmental of ourselves and to be loving and accepting of others. In order for you to truly be authentic and love you without condition, you must learn to give yourself compassion. While studying counseling in graduate school, I was introduced to a concept, *"Hold yourself kindly"*. That resonated with me and is my go to technique with not only myself but my clients. The premise behind this is we need to be kind(er) to ourselves, giving ourselves the emotional support, the "hug" and comfort needed when life happens. Self-compassion involves acting the same way toward yourself when you are having a difficult time or notice something you don't like about yourself, as you do when you achieve and make good choices. It's being kind to and understanding yourself when confronted with change, disappointments, and personal failings. It means recognizing that making a bad choice, doesn't mean you're a bad person. Self-compassion contains the attributes of "being with" ourselves in a compassionate way - comforting, soothing and validating. It's your inner coach, giving you the support and pep talk needed to pause and get back in the game.

> *"If you truly want to be remarkable you must first learn how to be yourself; this means living authentically and having a deep sense of who you are and what you have to offer." —Matt Russell*

The key requisites to cultivating self-love and self-acceptance are compassion, forgiveness and viewing yourself as someone evolving and growing. It's happily accepting your identity and uniqueness and knowing that it's a continuous gradual process that requires you to actively participate and commit. Authenticity is a practice, something you decide to do and be every day.

Embracing the authentic you means that you can't neglect or negate the "not-so-good" parts of you or your story. It requires vulnerability and a willingness to recognize and make peace with the "chapters" in the story you've denied, buried and skipped over. The authentic *you* is what makes you unique. It's how God created you, so don't deny your authentic self, embrace her. The *Authentic YOU* is ready to be released. Make room for her, the person you are becoming. Embrace her, honor her and reveal her.

Embracing you is about acceptance - accepting who you are, while still evolving.

REFLECTION

- What does embracing you look like?

- What parts of you are hard to accept and embrace?

- Complete the following sentence. I need to forgive myself for_____.

- Identify two ways you can begin celebrating how far you've come.

PRAYER

Lord, thank you for creating me with purpose and intent, for knowing my flaws and still loving me. For shaping and molding me. I am grateful for evolving and growth. Help me to see who you see and love myself as you do me. My desire is to embrace me in a new and powerful way Lord. Help me to be brave, vulnerable and committed to this process. The process of being authentic and of being compassionate to myself. I want to be confident in every area of my life and be able to show how you've helped me to heal. I embrace becoming who I truly am. Today I celebrate being thought of, being your masterpiece and all that you've created me to be. I honor my process and progress. I accept me, every part of me. I honor you and your spirit working inside of me. Have your way in my life. Amen.

PART FOUR

Leaning into Loving You

"Every day we choose between love and something else..."

Part Four

THIS THING CALLED LOVE

ATTTTTTT LAST, MY *love has come along*… did you read that in your Etta James voice? Hahaha! Finally, we've made it to this moment, the moment where we get to examine the last and most crucial part of us, how we *love*. So let's get right to it…How much do you truly love *yourself?* If I asked you to name all the things you love, I wonder how long it would take for you to name yourself? Why is it hard to love you?

The greatest travesty is that we can't see the value within. We place value and esteem on others, on things, and places, but rarely do we marvel at the wonders of ourselves. *Love yourself* they say, as if spewing the statement out will be a quick and magical process. These two words are the most difficult to hear, let alone grasp. They are loaded with so much, and there is so much left to interpretation. The concept will have you on a scavenger hunt for what seems like an eternity. I remember starting my own scavenger hunt of loving me. I had just recommitted my life to the Lord and desired more of Him, but there was something stopping me from fully being intimate with the Lord. Not understanding what the problem was, I became frustrated because I could feel the yearning to be closer and to be loved, but I wasn't sure how to get there. There were no directions or GPS to getting intimate with God, so I struggled.

For a very long time, I could only receive God on the surface. What I didn't know was that one of my deepest voids was I didn't feel loved nor did I know how to love. My formative years with love were not the greatest. I learned that in order to receive love, there was something *I* needed to do or be. As a result, I questioned love. Who loved me? Was it true? What if I no longer can do or be what they loved? Why wasn't I worthy of true love? I knew something was missing. I wasn't sure what I was "supposed" to experience, but love for me became more than a quest. It was something I needed to conquer, to achieve, and to have. Love was like my hidden treasure. I had a map (a figurative one I created), and I began digging, searching and trying desperately to find this four-letter word I had shaped my entire existence around. I saw others experience love from their parents, family members, and significant others and I began to long for it more and more. I envied them, the idea of what they had. The feelings plagued me. They ruled my every thought and my entire being. Obtaining love became my driving force; it was the reason behind almost every one of my actions. It was if I had signs on my face that said, "*Pick me! I am worthy of love, don't you see me?*". I allowed the quest to be more than the act.

The reason I couldn't fully receive love from God was because I had a distorted picture of love. My yearning and desire for love were tied up with far too many people and things, and I couldn't love me. I was lost in the pursuit of validation, perfection, and pretending. After several years of doing the work - the reflecting, the evaluating, the embracing - I was able to receive and embrace God's love and began learning new ways of loving myself. When we stop searching for a specific thing and look right in front of us, we'd see that what we were looking for was within us all along. I wanted so bad for others to treat me the way I wasn't treating myself. I spent far too many years on a quest to find LOVE when *I am* LOVE. Leaning into this concept and taking time to remove the false ideas and perceptions of what LOVE was, aided me in learning new ways to honor, value and love myself unconditionally. I learned that love is a deep appreciation and I need to accept and appreciate all of me. So do you. You owe it to yourself to fully experience YOU - the best, the worst, the embarrassing, the comical, the vulnerable – all parts that make you, *you*.

How we love and steward ourselves is the prerequisite for how other people treat us. Knowing how love manifests in your life will help you understand yourself more and learn new ways of loving yourself.

I want you to take a moment and think about the concept of love:

- What is your first understanding of love?
- Was this a healthy version? Was it a fairytale version? Did you think it was attainable?
- What has love told you?

Taking time to understand your perception of love, how you first understood it and how those perceptions show up in your thinking and actions now will help you navigate through the unrealistic responses you have with love.

Our relationship with self is one of the most important relationships we'll ever have. We're taught to put others first to cultivate meaningful, lasting relationships with everyone but ourselves. Oftentimes, we are the afterthought. You know what that means, after we've given our all to our careers, relationships, and our family, we are merely operating off what's left. Loving yourself is key to living the life you want and freeing yourself from the need to please others. It is time for you to be better with loving you. *Self-love* is the ability to be intentional about loving you. There are three types of self-love:

1. Physical - refers to how you see yourself.

2. Mental - refers to how you think of yourself.

3. Psychological - refers to how you treat yourself.

Self-love takes time and is a process, one that involves breaking down, shedding and removing thoughts, ideas, attitudes and things that do not serve us in our lives and do not fully reflect who we truly are. It means making it your highest priority to cultivate daily physical, mental, emotional and spiritual practices that will help you become everything God created you to be. It is both an attitude and an act; self-love is how you view yourself and how you live your life. It's a verb and requires action. It's the ability to ask yourself daily what you need and strive to receive it. Your life's mission is not to have a certain financial status, obtain more education or even make the world greater. Your life's mission is to become madly in love with the person God created, every single day and in turn, you will show up as your most authentic self. When you make this the mission, you can walk in your purpose, and you begin to love out loud. Loving yourself requires action, that you believe you deserve and are capable of staying true to yourself. It takes dedication, devotion, and determination.

LEANING IN

THERE IS A book written by Gary Chapman entitled "The 5 Love Languages" and is a book on how humans feel love. His idea is that there are five love languages. Along with this, we all have a hierarchy of love languages, and we mainly feel love in one or two of these categories. The five love languages are:

- Quality time
- Gifts
- Words of Affirmation
- Acts of service
- Physical touch

Knowing how you receive love is imperative to a healthy relationship. If you haven't done so, visit www.5lovelanguages.com/quizzes and be sure to take a moment to complete the love languages quiz and learn your love language. While the "5 Love Languages" is written to show you ways to love a spouse or loved one, I believe it is a great tool to strengthen and learn to care for your own love needs. Let's look at how you can incorporate your love language into your self-care.

5 Love Languages for Self-Love

If *Words of Affirmation (Speaking to YOU)* **is your primary love language** – It is important that you take time to uplift and honor yourself with your words. This can be intentionally taking time every day to say nice things to yourself. Practice daily declarations and speak over yourself, because we know that our words are life forming and precede our emotions and behaviors. This can be done during your morning routine while brushing your teeth or in the shower. You can tell yourself 2-3 things that you value and love about yourself. It's maintaining positive self-talk and showing yourself kindness.

If *Acts of Service (Doing things for YOU)* **is your primary love language** – You'll want to do what makes you come alive and feel loved. It's performing acts of service for yourself, look at ways to fill your heart with joy. It can be preparing yourself healthy meals, taking time to care for yourself and serve your body well. It's nurturing actions and acts of independence.

If *Receiving Gifts (Giving to yourself)* **is your primary love language** – you'll want to purchase tangible tokens of appreciation and appreciation for yourself. You can set aside a certain amount of money per week, whatever you can afford, to buy yourself something that you have always wanted. Gift yourself an experience or invest in a hobby. It's about making purchases that increase your quality of life.

If *Quality Time (Being Present with yourself)* **is your primary love language** – your focus is intentionally spending time with you, doing something that fills you with joy and relieves stress. It's making you a priority and dedicating time of solitude ("me-time") and reflection regularly.

If *Physical Touch* (*Feeling*) **is your primary love language** - it means that you must show yourself love through physical touch. It's feeling self-love and connecting with yourself. Having physical displays of affection, body awareness and learning what makes you feel good are all a part of this. You could get a massage, a manicure or pedicure.

Whatever your self-love language may be, start today by making yourself a priority and resolve to commit to loving you in a new and intentional way, with no apologies.

UNAPOLOGETICALLY YOU

HOW MANY TIMES have you apologized for being you? Think about how many times you've said "I'm sorry" for non-offensive behavior? "I'm sorry, but can we reschedule our lunch?", "*I'm sorry*, but can I say something?", "I am sorry but...". Statistics show that women apologize for almost everything in their personal and professional lives. We apologize way too much for being who we are and choosing ourselves. We have a tendency to feel bad for taking time out for us, for showing up greater for ourselves than we do anyone else, and the list goes on. Our behaviors can be apologetic for achieving high levels of success. We don't want to seem "boastful" or too smart, so we shrink back. Stop apologizing for being you! You worked hard to become this version of yourself and it's time you own it! Loving you means that you make no apologies for your strengths, your weaknesses, your desires, and for the essence of who you are. It means standing firm in your decisions, not compromising. Being unapologetically you means that you know exactly who you are, what you stand for and what you will not stand for. Being unapologetic about your life, your needs, desires, values and success means living free of shame, guilt and apologies for who you truly are. When you are confident in who you are, make no apologies for it. You owe it to yourself to live a bold, bright, and beautiful life.

Part Four

"Trust is the glue of life. It's the most essential ingredient in effective communication. It's the foundational principle that holds all relationships"

- Stephen Covey

TRUST YOURSELF

THE FACT THAT there are millions of women who don't believe they are trustworthy of their own choices is disheartening. We as women second guess ourselves, shrink back and live in constant fear due to trust issues and most of those issues are with ourselves. I don't quite remember when I began doubting me, but I know it caused me to play small for far too many years. It could have been that time in high school when I told myself that I wasn't good enough for student government but I knew I had the gift and intellect. Or maybe it was the time I decided to shrink back in my career because I was scared of how great I would become and I didn't trust myself to handle it all.

When did you stop trusting you? What happened that made you doubt you and your abilities? Trust is the heartbeat of every significant relationship, and it is no different for you. Every one of us is born with an inner skill or resource that if nurtured and cultivated properly allows us to be self-reliant and trust our decisions. Don't believe me? Take a moment to watch a child play and live carefree, trusting their choices and taking risks. While we start out in life with a strong sense of self-trust, as we grow and go through life, we become conditioned to seek approval and validation from others instead of ourselves, which causes us to doubt ourselves, and our choices.

There is still that part of you that knows what to do in every situation, but it is usually silenced with your thoughts and lack of confidence within. Self-trust is reliance on the integrity, strength and ability of oneself. It means that you trust yourself to never give up on you, to survive circumstances. It means that you rely on the God inside of you to help you navigate life. Self-trust is our personal power that God gave each of us to operate and fulfill our destiny. Building trust within yourself starts with keeping promises and your commitments to you. It's honoring your word to you and being who you said you'd be for yourself, no matter how you feel, because it requires action.

Self-trust is a valuable asset to your journey of self-love and is developed by nurturing our innermost thoughts, and is built with consistency. Self-trust requires faith - faith in yourself, your judgments, choices, and abilities. Developing self-trust also includes becoming a better friend to you and building habits that support your dreams, goals and values. Asking yourself the hard questions and learning the truths will help you develop trust again.

Questions have power – great power, and if you address yourself with simple yet deep and honest questions, you will get the answers needed to activate the power to have great faith in yourself and your abilities. Knowing and loving yourself produces trust. As soon as you begin trusting in yourself, you open up space to love you authentically.

BENEFITS OF LOVING YOU

THE RELATIONSHIP WITH you is ever changing and growing and is the best gift you'll ever give yourself. While it is one of the hardest relationships you'll ever build, self-love can make positive and impactful change in your life. There are thousands of benefits of loving you, here are a few:

1. You no longer live as a victim but as a champion.

2. You show up in the world as your authentic self and live out your God-given purpose.

3. You allow yourself to be human and release yourself from perfection. Accepting your flaws, mistakes and failures.

4. You invite vulnerability in, and let go of shame, blame and anger.

5. You value your existence and honor God's thoughts of you.

6. You develop emotional security.

7. You embrace self-compassion.

8. You cultivate inner strength and peace.

9. You become a risk taker.

10. You activate your personal power.

CELEBRATION IS IN ORDER

IT IS TIME for you to celebrate you. You have celebrated everyone and everything over the years. You've gone to the parties, purchased the gifts, created the posts to highlight and celebrate the people in your life that are doing amazing things and rightfully so, but what about you, my dear? When are you going to take a moment to honor you? Now, don't get me wrong, I believe we definitely should honor and celebrate the people in our lives, as we have been…but this book is about you, not them. I'm not talking about huge moments because it's easy to celebrate the new car, the new boo, the house, the promotion, the graduation, etc. And while those big moments deserve celebrating, stop neglecting the small but impactful strides *you've* made to get to this very moment. When was the last time you stopped and took a moment to celebrate and reward you? How about right now, for actually doing the work and cultivating you? It's time to celebrate - celebrate where you are, and the season that you are in. Celebrate the strides you've made even if those strides are only one or two steps, or just mean that you've literally gotten up off the floor or out of your "low place." It is reflecting on how far you've come. So often we are in a rush to get to the new place. We're in such a rush to evolve, to grow, to get out of the uncomfortable place, that we don't take moments to reflect on the strength it took to get to *this* place, even if *this* place is in the same room just a different space. The relationship with self is ever changing, growing and requires nurturing and cultivation. It's never too late or early to begin honoring and celebrating you. Commit to celebrating who you are and make it a habit to toot your own horn. You deserve it and loving yourself means that you celebrate your very existence. Whatever celebrating looks like for you... **DO IT!**

\

SAY HELLO TO YOU

CULTIVATING AND LOVING the authentic you is not easy, as you have come to realize, but it is powerful and allows you to live beyond self-imposed limits of your heart and mind. It allows you to embrace the evolution of yourself and celebrate the progress along the way. When you cultivate self-love, you decide to no longer dodge the reflection you see in the mirror because you embrace every part of her. You make no apologies about who you are and what you've been through. You trust yourself and your capabilities. It is a beautiful process similar to the butterfly.

The butterfly begins its life going through stages of growth and transformation. It begins as a larva, then a pupa, and then it becomes the familiar, caterpillar. The caterpillar then undergoes the process called Metamorphosis. Metamorphosis brings about a dramatic change in character or appearance of those who go through it. Metamorphosis is about evolution, change, and transformation. It is about making corrections at any point in time in your life, to embrace, align, and adjust. Unlike the caterpillar, our transformation isn't in the body but in our minds. It's how we see ourselves, how we speak and develop. Paul challenges us to experience

---

metamorphosis in **Romans 12:2** when he says, *"Do not conform to the pattern of this world but be transformed by the renewing of your mind. Then you will be able to test and approve what God's will is—His good, pleasing and perfect will."*

The power of experiencing metamorphosis (transformation) is that you get to re-introduce yourself to the person you've evolved into. It's time to look again, not at the caterpillar you've once seen in the mirror, but say hello to the beautiful butterfly that has emerged from life's experiences. With HELLO being one of the most simple yet powerful gestures, it symbolizes an introduction. Because so much has happened in your life, it's time to introduce yourself to the newest version of you. It's time to start saying HELLO:

- Saying HELLO is embracing your transformation, your personal metamorphosis. It's acknowledging that you have undergone significant change.

- Saying HELLO is deciding to learn you continually.

- Saying HELLO is bravely embracing the new version of you.

- Saying HELLO is celebrating your life where you are, what you've survived and also what's coming.

- Saying HELLO is giving yourself permission to be a work in progress.

- Saying HELLO is knowing there is more in front of you than there is behind you.

Are ready to meet the love of your life?

Look no further, here she is...SAY,

HELLO ME!

*"We ask ourselves, who am I to be
brilliant, gorgeous, talented and fabulous?
Actually, who are you not to be? You
are a child of God. Your playing small
doesn't serve the world. There's nothing
enlightened about shrinking so that other
people won't feel insecure around you.*

*We were born to manifest the glory of
God that is within us. It's not just in
some of us; it's in everyone. And as we
let our own light shine, we unconsciously
give other people permission to do the
same. As we are liberated from our own
fear, our presence automatically liberates
others".*
~Marianne Williamson

REFLECTION

Leaning into and learning new ways of loving you requires that you become vulnerable with you. Think about what you've learned so far:

- What ways can you begin to implement the lesson?

- What has love taught you?

- What is your greatest victory so far?

- Today I am leaning more into loving myself by_____?

- List three ways you will begin trusting yourself more

- Take time to go back and highlight key points, tools and "aha" moments and begin journaling your thoughts.

- What is your biggest takeaway from this book?

- One thing you can't wait to share and discuss with your friends?

PRAYER

Lord, thank you for loving me when I didn't even love myself. It takes a lot for me to see myself beyond my flaws and faults, but I am learning. Thank you for showing me; me. For the tools to honor myself and to show up in a vulnerable way that celebrates my imperfections and growth. Teach me how to continuously be unapologetic about who I am, your daughter, the one you thought of before the foundations of the earth. I stand leaning into the greatest parts of me, while working on the not so great parts. Father help me to live life being my truest self, loving and accepting myself, my body, and my heart. Let your love break all the lies I have told myself, help me to reprogram my mind that I may embrace my authentic and most powerful self. Lord, I desire to be ME, no one else but the person you created. I walk boldly as myself and I compare myself to no one from this day forward. Align me with the vision you have for my life Lord and help me to fully embrace your plans for my life. Today is my new beginning, I start my life over seeing myself in a new way with compassion, acceptance, love and adoration. Thank You father for allowing me to say hello to me. It's in Jesus name I pray Amen.

LET'S KEEP TALKING

This book teaches you to develop an authentic relationship with yourself and provides the tools to challenge your view of self, your thinking, comfort levels, and actions considering how you treat yourself. The reason I started the **Hello** series is that there are far too many women not living a life of self-assurance and authenticity. The bigger problem is that lack of self-awareness, self-love, and authenticity doesn't just affect one area of your live, it affects every area, causing you, your family, your friends, and the kingdom of God to suffer as a result.

The goal of this book has been to assist you in cultivation and embracing who you are, and this is not the end of the conversation, but the beginning. The beginning of you unveiling and unleashing your most powerful self and ultimately your transformation will evoke change for everyone in your life because while this book was for you, it is beyond you. I ask that you commit to telling at least fifty of your family, friends, and associates about it and encourage them to purchase the book (and not borrow yours) or consider gifting it to them and allow the life-changing experience to transform their life too.

I also invite you to continue the discussion with me by joining my community the Purpose Crew at www.madeforpurpose.org. Let's keep talking about these issues and supporting one another.

Thank you

Additional Resources

Email hello@madeforpurpose.org for a free 5-day HELLO ME prayer and devotional.

ABOUT THE AUTHOR

I'M YAH HUGHES, The Purpose Cultivator ™. My purpose and greatest joys are seeing women become their most authentic self and live a life of purpose and intention. As a Christian Coach, I help women shift their relationship with painful experiences, emotions & excuses, develop a new mindset and walk in purpose.

With more than **15 years' experience** as a trainer, higher education professional, and emotional wholeness coach, I specialize in working with women who are tired of going in cycles, living with pain, fear, doubt, and are ready to GET UP out of their low places to walk in purpose. I am the CEO and Founder of **Made for Purpose** a personal and self-development business. Holding a Master of Education in Community Counseling, I couple my formal education, professional training, and experiences with biblical principles to work with you to explore what is possible in life, gain clarity/focus and change unhealthy life patterns.

I am the proud author of *Made Whole: A Woman's Journey from Painful to Purposeful*. A life-changing account of how I traded fear for faith, doubt for destiny and pain for purpose and also *You Need It, I Got It : Conversations with Global Entrepreneurs on Growing Your Audience, Visibility & Influence...* which gained me the acclaimed title of 2x **Best Selling Author** (Emotional Help and Women & Business).

While all of this brings me joy, my greatest joy is being a wife to my incredible husband and mother to my two children.

REFERENCES

Martin, S. (2016). 26 questions to help you know yourself better

Becoming A Butterfly! — Inspiritual." Insert Name of Site in Italics. N.p., n.d. Web. 08 May. 2019 https://www.inspiritual.biz/inspiritual-reflections/2012/11/26/becoming-a-butter.

Our Deepest Fear Is Not That We Are Inadequate, By ... (n.d.). Retrieved from http://skdesigns.com/internet/articles/quotes/williamson/our_deepest_fear/

Colletti, F. (2015). How MSPs can add value through reporting. Channel Pro, n/a.

Toni Collette Quotes - Brainyquote." Insert Name of Site in Italics. N.p., n.d. Web. 08 May. 2019 https://www.brainyquote.com/quotes/toni_collette_432032.

Toni Collette Quotes - Brainyquote." Insert Name of Site in Italics. N.p., n.d. Web. 08 May. 2019 https://www.brainyquote.com/quotes/toni_collette_432032.

References

References

Made in the USA
Middletown, DE
15 October 2023